Dickinson John

A Speech, Delivered in the House of Assembly of the

Province of Pennsylvania

May 24th, 1764

Dickinson John

A Speech, Delivered in the House of Assembly of the Province of Pennsylvania
May 24th, 1764

ISBN/EAN: 9783337149802

Printed in Europe, USA, Canada, Australia, Japan

Cover: Foto ©ninafisch / pixelio.de

More available books at **www.hansebooks.com**

A

S P E E C H,

DELIVERED IN

The HOUSE of ASSEMBLY

Of the Province of PENNSYLVANIA,

MAY 24th, 1764.

By JOHN DICKINSON, Efq;

One of the MEMBERS for the County of *Philadelphia*.

On Occafion of a PETITION, drawn up by Order, and then under Confideration, of the *Houfe* ; praying his *Majefty* for a Change of the *Government* of this *Province*.

WITH

A PREFACE.

Certe ego libertatem, quæ mihi a Parente meo tradita eft, experiar; verum id fruftra, an ob rem faciam, in veftra manu fitum ift, Quirites.
SALL. Bell. Jugurth. in Orat. MEMMII.

As for me, I will affuredly contend for that glorious plan of *Liberty* handed down to us from our anceftors ; but whether my Labours fhall prove fuccefsful, or in vain, depends wholly on you, my dear Countrymen !

PHILADELPHIA Printed:

LONDON,
Re-Printed for J. WHISTON and B. WHITE, in *Fleet-ftreet.*
M.DCC.LXIV.

PREFACE.

TO underſtand clearly the nature of that diſpute which led the Aſſembly to thoſe meaſures, which are ſo juſtly animadverted on in the following excellent Speech, it will be proper to look a few years backward.

In the year 1759, Governor D———, whoſe adminiſtration will never be mentioned but with diſgrace in the annals of this Province, was induced, by conſiderations to which the world is now no ſtranger, to paſs ſundry acts, contrary to his duty, and to every tie of honor and juſtice. On the 2d of September 1760, his late Majeſty in council repealed ſix of theſe acts; and in regard to the 7th (which was an act for granting to his Majeſty One hundred thouſand Pounds, by a tax on all eſtates real and perſonal, &c.) the Lords of his Majeſty's moſt honourable Privy Council declared it their opinion, " that the ſaid act was fundamentally WRONG and UNJUST, and ought to be repealed, unleſs ſix certain amendments were made therein ;"———.

BENJAMIN FRANKLIN and Robert Charles, Agents for the Province, undertook that, in caſe the act might be left unrepealed, " the Aſſembly of Pennſylvania would prepare and paſs an act for making the amendments propoſed by the Lords of the Council, and to indemnify the Proprietaries from any damage they might ſuſtain by ſuch an act not being prepared and paſſed. This ſtipulation was ſigned by the hands of the ſaid agents, and the Proprietors for the ſake of peace accepted of it.

BUT

But, notwithstanding the solemnity of this agreement, the Assembly, in framing the late *Supply-Bill*, insisted upon explaining the 2d and 3d articles of the stipulation in their own way, and inserting them in the bill in different words from those made use of by the Lords of Council, and signed by their own agents. The Governor, on the contrary, thought that no words could be so proper to convey the meaning of the Lords of Council and prevent disputes, as those which their Lordships themselves had made use of; and that he could neither in decency or duty depart from them.

Hereupon messages ensued, and the Assembly, among other vehement and warm resolves, broke up with the following most extraordinary one, *viz.*

" That this House will adjourn, in order to consult their constituents, whether an humble address should be drawn up, and transmitted to his Majesty, praying, that he would be graciously pleased to take the people of this province, under his immediate protection and government, &c."

What methods were taken, during this adjournment, to lead a number of rash, ignorant, and inconsiderate people into petitions, the evil tendency of which they did not understand, is an enquiry not suitable to the present occasion. It is enough to say, that, after incredible pains, in a Province containing near THREE HUNDRED THOUSAND SOULS, not more than 3500 could be prevailed upon to petition for a change of government; and those very generally of a low rank, many of whom could neither read nor write.

The wiser and better part of the province had far different notions of this measure. They considered that the moment they put their hands to these petitions,
they

they might be furrendering up their birth-right, and putting it in the power of a few men, for the fake of gratifying their own ambitious projects and perfonal refentments, to barter away that glorious plan of public liberty and charter privileges, under which this Province has rifen to the higheft degree of profperity, with a rapidity almoft unparalleled in hiftory.

Though the ill fuccefs of thefe petitions muft have been very mortifying to the projectors of them, yet the Affembly were, at all hazards, to be perfuaded to make them the foundation of a petition to the King for a change of government. It was in vain to urge the fmallnefs of the numbers who figned the petitions; the high veneration in which our prefent conftitution hath long been held by good men of every denomination, and the multitudes of induftrious people whom even the very fame of it hath invited among us, from almoft every part of the world. Thefe confiderations were but flight bars to men actuated by ambition and refentment; men, who have long found their own importance to confift in fomenting the divifions of their country, and now hope to aggrandize themfelves by bringing about the propofed change, whatever may be its confequences to others. They therefore found means to carry their petition through the Houfe; but not without the moft fpirited teftimony againft it, from a NOBLE FEW, a Patriot Minority, whofe names will be mentioned with honor, fo long as any remembrance is left of the prefent boafted LIBERTIES of PENNSILVANIA.

At the head of thefe Few, the worthy author of the following Speech fignalized himfelf. Having devoted to a fevere courfe of ftudy thofe years which too many give to diffipation and pleafure, he fhewed himfelf, at his firft entrance on public life, poffeffed of a knowledge of the laws and conftitution of his country,

which

which feldom falls to the fhare even of grey hairs. Alike independent in fpirit and in fortune, removed as far as any man can be from all connexions with the Proprietors or their immediate friends, and following only the unbiaffed dictates of his own heart ; he could not be a filent fpectator while the moft diftant attempt was made upon that conftitution, for which our fathers planted a wildernefs, and which is derived to us by the FAITH OF CHARTERS, and SANCTITY OF LAWS !

THIS SPEECH was delivered on the 24th of May, and the late Speaker, Mr. NORRIS, with the four Members under-mentioned, are faid to have declared to Mr. DICKINSON, that he had fully fpoke their Sentiments, in his own. The next day in the afternoon, Mr. Dickinfon *moved* that the further confideration of the matter fhould be adjourned to the following morning. But it was voted by a great majority (Mr. Dickinfon, Mr. Jofeph Richardfon, Mr. Ifaac Saunders, and Mr. John Montgomery being for the negative) that the PETITION, as then drawn, fhould be tranfcribed, in order to be figned by the Speaker ; which was ordered accordingly.

MR. Dickinfon having then digefted the heads of his fpeech into the nature of a *Proteft*, in which he was joined by Mr. Saunders and Mr Montgomery *, offered it to be entered in the minutes ; but it was refufed.

MR. NORRIS the Speaker, who, from the nature of his office, could not join in the *Proteft* or take any part in the debate, finding matters pufhed to this extremity, informed the Houfe, in a very folemn and affecting manner, " That for thirty years paft he had had the honour of ferving as a Reprefentative of the

* See their letter below.

people

people of this Province, and near half that time as SPEAKER——That, in thefe offices, he had uniformly endeavoured, according to the beft of his judgment, to promote the public good——That the fubject of the prefent debate was a matter of the utmoft importance to the Province—That, as his fentiments on the occafion were very different from thofe of the *majority*, and his feat in the chair prevented him from entering into the debate, he therefore *prayed* the Houfe, That if, in confequence of their order, his duty fhould oblige him to fign the *Petition* as Speaker, he might be permitted to offer his fentiments on the fubject before he figned, and that they might be entered on the minutes ;" which was granted accordingly.

THE Houfe then adjourned to the next morning, and when they met, the Clerk delivered the members a letter from the *Speaker*, acquainting them that his indifpofition prevented his further attendance, and praying them to chufe a new Speaker. Thus this aged member and faithful fervant of the Houfe, as if forefeeing troubles to come, chofe to retire, and leave them to thofe whofe temper they better fuited.

BENJAMIN FRANKLIN, Efq; was *accordingly* chofen *Speaker*, and in the afternoon of the fame day, figned the *Petition*, as one of his firft acts; an act which * * * but pofterity will beft be able to give it a name ?

As thefe tranfactions could not fail of being very interefting to the good people of this Province, it is not to be wondered that they expreffed an earneft defire to fee the following *Speech*, that they might be able to form fome knowledge of what was intended : for their own Reprefentatives did not think proper to let the contents of their petition for the propofed change be known; tho' upon this fingle ftake, fo far as depended upon them, they have rifqued our whole conftitution. On

4

the

the 6th of June, therefore, a great number of the principal Gentlemen of *Philadelphia*, applied to Mr Dickinson for a copy of his speech, by letter as follows *viz.*

" *Philadelphia, June 6th,* 1764.

" S I R,

WE whose names are underwritten, citizens of Philadelphia, acknowledge the obligations that the good people of this Province are under to you, for your spirited defence of our charter privileges, which we apprehend are greatly endangered by some late proceedings, particularly the setting on foot a petition to his Majesty for a change of government. We are surprized that our representatives, who ought to be guardians of the constitution, do not check rather than encourage this unseasonable application of a few (comparatively) of the people of this extensive Province. We hereby testify our sincere gratitude to you, Sir, and the other patriot Members that appeared on the side of our Charter and Privileges, and request a copy of the Speech you delivered on that occasion in the House, as we are perswaded that the publication thereof would be of great utility, and give general satisfaction. We beg leave to assure you of our regard, and are,

S I R,

Your most obedient

Humble Servants."

ABOUT

ABOUT the fame time Mr. *Saunders* and Mr. *Montgo-mery*, earneftly defirous that their names might be join-ed with Mr. *Dickinfon's* thro' this whole affair, fent him the following letter.

" S I R,

AS we are informed that a number of the principal gentlemen of the city of Philadelphia intend ap-plying to you to have your Speech, which was deliver'd a few days ago in the Houfe of Affembly, againft the meafures propofed for a change of government, pub-lifhed ; and as we are of opinion the publication thereof, together with the reafons on which our proteft is found-ed, may be of confiderable fervice : We judge it pro-per (in cafe you are of the fame opinion of making them publick) that you fhould fignify to the publick how heartily we have concurred with you in the fame fenti-ments, fet forth in your Speech, and in difapprobation of the late refolves of the Houfe ; this we judge a piece of juftice due to ourfelves, leaft we incurr, from our confti-tuents, the imputation of betraying or facrificing their effential rights and privileges which we meant to de-fend : We likewife authorize you hereby to affix our names to the diffent and proteft*, which the Houfe re-fufed entering on their minutes.   We are refpectfully,

Sir,   *Your's &c.*

ISAAC SAUNDERS.

JOHN MONTGOMERY."

* As all the arguments in this *Proteft* are to be found more at large in the following Speech, it is not printed here, but will be publifhed by itfelf in the News Papers.

b   HAVING

HAVING thus given a faithful account, both of the occasion of this Speech, and of its publication, it would be almost impossible not to quote a few passages from former Assemblies, to shew in what high terms, even of rapture and admiration, they continually mentioned our present constitution and plan of government.

" WE hope, say they *, the people of Pennsylvania will never be wanting to acknowlege the great wisdom and singular goodness of our late honourable Proprietor, from whom we derive the privileges of our annual elections, as well as many other immunities, which have so manifestly contributed to the prosperity of the Province, &c." Again,

" WHEN † we commemorate the many blessings bestowed on the inhabitants of this colony, the *religious* and *civil liberties* we possess, and to whom these valuable blessings, under God and the King, are owing, we should be wanting to ourselves, and them that we represent, did we not do justice to the memory of thy worthy ancestor".

" Our ‡ happy constitution, secured to us by the wisdom and goodness of our first Proprietary and founder of this province, so happily continued to us under the government of his honourable descendants, justly entitle them to our affection and zeal for their honour and interest."

BUT it would be endless to quote all that has been said by our Assemblies, in favour of the constitution of this province, and its worthy founder. The sum of the whole, when taken from the minutes, and thrown together in their own express words, is nothing less than what follows.

* Assembly 1730.
† Address to the honourable JOHN PENN, Esq; 1764.
‡ Assembly 1738.

WILLIAM

WILLIAM PENN,

(1) A man of principles truely humane,
an Advocate for
Religion and Liberty,
(2) *Poſſeſſing* a noble ſpirit
That exerted itſelf
For the good of mankind,
Was
(3) The great and worthy founder
Of
Pennsylvania.
To its Inhabitants, by Charter,
(4) He granted and confirmed
(5) Many ſingular Privileges and Immunities,
(6) Civil and Religious ;
(7) Which he continually ſtudied
to preſerve and defend for them,
Nobly declaring
(8) That they had not followed him ſo far
To loſe a ſingle tittle
Of the Great Charter
To which all *Engliſhmen* were born !
For theſe Services,
(9) Great have been the acknowledgements
Deſervedly paid to his Merit ;
(10) And his Memory
Is dear to his people,
Who have repeatedly confeſſed
That,
(11) Next to divine Providence,
(12) Their Happineſs, Proſperity and Increaſe
(13) Are owing
To his wiſe conduct and ſingular goodneſs,
(14) Which deſerve ever to be remembered,

(1) Minutes 1734.   (5) Minutes 1730.   (10) Minutes 1719.
(2) Minutes 1740.   (6) Minutes 1734.   (11) Minutes 1725.
(3) Minutes 1738.   (7) Minutes 1735.   (12) Minutes 1731.
    1740, 1745.   (8) Minutes 1756,   (13) Minutes 1734.
(4) Minutes 1755.   (9) Minutes 1740.   (14) Minutes 1732.

                                             With

With
GRATITUDE and AFFECTION,
By PENNSYLVANIANS.

WERE it intended to write the higheft encomium
on the conftitution of this country, and to erect the
moft lafting monument to the memory of its illuftrious founder, a more noble *infcription* could hardly be
devifed than what is contained in the foregoing minutes of Affembly : and a time may come, when
impartial pofterity, notwithftanding the prefent in-
gratitude of a *few*, may perhaps adapt it for this purpofe.

As to the wild meafures now on foot, they will undoubtedly deftroy themfelves by their own violence ;
and it would be impoffible to add any thing that can
more expofe their rafhnefs than what is contained in
the following Speech. The Proprietors hold *their
Right* by that charter under which ours is derived.
Can the latter in law or equity be deemed more facred
than the former ? Have the Proprietors, by any act
of theirs, forfeited the leaft tittle of what was granted
them by his Majefty's royal anceftors ? Or can they
be deprived of their charter-rights without their own
confent ? have they not conftantly fheltered themfelves under the wing of government, and received
the approbation of his Majefty's firft fervants in the
law to every material *Inftruction* fent to their governors
here ?

IN the prefent difpute nothing has been infifted
upon on the part of our Governors but a ftrict adherence to what has been folemnly determined by his
Majefty in Council.

INDEED we have every way the worft of this whole
bufinefs. If a change were to take place, the Proprietors

prietors, before they refign their charter, would certainly obtain a full equivalent for their *Rights* of *Government*, and likewife have all their *Rights* of *Property* fecured to them by laws which we could not difpute. Such a change, were they inclined to it, could
certainly be of very little prejudice to them ; but with
refpect to us the cafe is quite different. Inftead of
fecuring any thing in reverfion or exchange, our reprefentatives, by their prefent petition, feem (fo far
at leaft as depends on them) to have offered up our
whole charter-rights, leaving it to the grace of others
to return us any part, or indeed no part of them,
according as it may be thought proper. But, thanks
be to God, this is a power with which our reprefentatives were never vefted by us ; and therefore the act
they have committed is VOID in itfelf. Nor is there
any doubt but an immenfe majority of the good people
of this Province will ftill be found ready, at a proper
time, to vindicate their charter-rights ; and to let the
world know that they hold thofe men unworthy of
all future truft, who could wantonly fport with things
fo facred.

FORMER Affemblies made it an article of impeach-
ment againft one of the moft confiderable * men of
this Province, " That he had contrived to violate
(only) a part of the conftitution of this government."
But what would they have thought of an attempt to
violate the whole ?

WE know it will be replied, that the change now
propofed is not a violation of this kind, and that our
privileges might be preferved in virtue of our *Laws*,
eeen if our charter were given up. But a fufficient
anfwer is given to this in page the 11th and 12th of
the following *Speech* ; and indeed it is aftonifhing. that

* James Logan, Efq;

this

this argument could ever be made ufe of to impofe upon any perfon, when it is well known that the chief privileges, by which the conftitution of this province is diftinguifhed, depend upon our charter alone, and upon no pofitive law whatever.

AND here, let no wrong conftruction be put upon this defence of the particular conftitution of *Pennfilva-nia*. Thofe who now contend for. it, have the high-eft veneration for the dignity and authority of the Crown. They think themfelves as much under its immediate protection as any of his Majefty's fubjects on this continent are ; and it is well known, that they have on all occafions been among the firft of thofe who have appeared in defence of the juft rights of our gracious Sovereign.

THEY think it may be faid, without giving the leaft offence, that the inhabitants of this Province enjoy certain privileges which are not to be found in the governments around them, and which they could not have the leaft hopes of preferving in cafe of any change of our prefent conftitution. Multitudes of people have chofen a fettlement in this Province, pre-ferable to all others, on account of thefe privileges ; and they now think that they have a right to the per-petual enjoyment of them : as they are in no cafe in-confiftent with good order or the public good. Many private corporations, in his Majefty's dominions, enjoy fingular immunities upon the like foundation ; and thofe bodies have never been thought undutiful for ad-hering tenacioufly to their rights, from age to age. Certainly we may be confidered in a fomething higher light than Corporate Bodies of this kind.

HAVING fwelled this preface to a much greater length than was at firft intended, we fhall only offer one remark more, upon the terms in which the *Pe-*

I   *tition*

tition of our Affembly is faid to be drawn up. We have heard that this Province is defcribed in it as a fcene of *riot, violence and confufion*; but yet one can hardly judge it poffible, that our reprefentatives could venture to approach the royal ear with fuch an unjuft account of their conftituents. Neverthelefs we have a right to infift on a copy of this petition from the Committee in whofe hands it is, that, if we lie under any accufations in it, we may have an opportunity to anfwer them. This is fo reafonable, that we are perfuaded it cannot be refufed, efpecially in a matter wherein we may be greatly affected.

We would only obferve, that the prefent is not a time for divifions of any kind in his Majefty's colonies; but for the clofeft union among ourfelves, that we may be able, by decent and juft reprefentations of the ftate of our country, to fave it from burthens which it cannot bear, and to encourage it in thofe improvements whereof it is capable. Let it be remembered how little we have got by bringing our party quarrels before the Crown thefe many years paft; moft certainly nothing but fhame to ourfelves, and a load of expence to our country, which, however beneficial it may have been to the *Agents* employed, has not been of the leaft fervice to the public.

THE

THE

S P E E C H

O F

JOHN DICKINSON, Efq; &c.

Mr. SPEAKER,

WHEN honeſt men apprehend their country to be injured, nothing is more natural than to reſent and complain : but when they enter into conſideration of the means for obtaining redreſs, the ſame virtue that gave the alarm, may ſometimes, by cauſing too great a tranſport of zeal, defeat its own purpoſe ; it being expedient for thoſe who deliberate of public affairs, that their minds ſhould be free from all violent paſſions. Theſe emotions blind the underſtanding : they weaken the judgment. It therefore frequently happens, that reſolutions formed by men thus agitated, appear to *them* very wiſe, very juſt, and very ſalutary ; while others, not influenced by the ſame heats, condemn thoſe determinations, as weak, unjuſt, and dangerous. Thus, Sir, in councils it will always be found uſeful, to guard againſt even that indignation, which ariſes from integrity.

A   MORE

MORE particularly are *we* bound to obferve the utmoft caution in our conduct, as the experience of
many years may convince us, that all our actions un-
dergo the ftrictett fcrutiny.——Numerous are the in-
ftances, that might be mentioned, of rights vindicated
and equitable demands made in this province, according to the opinions entertained here, that in *Great-
Britain* have been adjudged to be illegal attempts,
and pernicious pretenfions.

THESE adjudications are the acts of perfons vefted
with fuch dignity and power, as claim fome deference
from us : and hence it becomes not unneceffary to confider in what light the meafures now propofed may appear to thofe, whofe fentiments, from the conftitution
of our government, it will always be prudent to regard.

BUT on this important occafion, we ought not to
aim only at the approbation of men, whofe authority
may cenfure and controul us. More affecting duties
demand our attention. The honour and welfare of
Pennfylvania depending on our decifions, let us endea-
vour fo to act, that we may enjoy our own approbation, in the cool and undifturbed hours of reflexion ;
that we may deferve the approbation of the impartial
world ; and of pofterity, who are fo much interefted in
the prefent debate.

No man, Sir, can be more clearly convinced than
I am, of the inconveniences arifing from a ftrict adherence to proprietary inftructions. We are prevented
from demonftrating our loyalty to our excellent Sovereign, and our affection to our diftreft fellow-fubjects,
unlefs we will indulge the Proprietors, with a diftinct
and partial mode of taxation, by which they will fave
perhaps four or five hundred pounds a year, that ought
to go in eafe of our conftituents.

THIS

THIS is granted on all fides to be unequal; and has therefore excited the refentment of this Houfe. Let us refent——but let our refentment bear proportion to the provocation received; and not produce, or even expofe us to the peril of producing, effects more fatal than the injury of which we complain. If the change of government now meditated can take place, with all our privileges preferved; let it inflantly take place: but if *they* muft be confumed in the blaze of royal authority, we fhall pay too great a price for our approach to the throne; too great a price for obtaining (if we fhould obtain) the addition of four or five hundred pounds to the proprietary tax; or indeed for any emolument likely to follow from the change.

I HOPE I am not miftaken, when I believe that every member in this Houfe feels the fame reverence that I do, for thefe *ineftimable rights*. When I confider the fpirit of liberty that breathes in them, and the flourifhing ftate to which this province hath rifen in a few years under them, I am extremely defirous, that they fhould be tranfmitted to future ages; and I cannot fupprefs my folicitude, while fteps are taking, that tend to bring them all into danger. Being affured, that this houfe will always think an attempt to change this government too hazardous, unlefs thefe privileges can be *perfectly fecured*, I fhall beg leave to mention the reafons by which I have been convinced, that fuch an attempt ought not *now* to be made.

IT feems to me, Sir, that a people who intend an innovation of their government, ought to chufe the moft proper *time*, and the moft proper *method* for accomplifhing their purpofes; and ought ferioufly to weigh all the probable and poffible *confequences* of fuch a meafure.

THERE

THERE are certain periods in public affairs, when defigns may be executed much more eafily and advantageoufly, than at any other. It hath been by a ftrict attention to every interefting circumftance ; a careful cultivation of every fortunate occurrence; and patiently waiting till they have ripened into a favourable conjuncture, that fo many great actions have been performed in the political world.

IT was through a rafh neglect of this prudence, and too much *eagernefs* to gain his point, that the Duke of *Monmouth* deftroyed his own enterprize, and brought himfelf difhonourably to the block, though every thing then verged towards a revolution.
The Prince of Orange with a *wife delay* purfued the fame views, and glorioufly mounted a throne.

IT was through a like neglect of this prudence, that the commons of *Denmark*, fmarting under the tyranny of their nobility, in a fit of revengeful fury, *fuddenly* furrendered their liberties to the king ; and ever fince, with unavailing grief and ufelefs execrations, have detefted the *mad moment*, which flipt upon them the fhackles of flavery, which no ftruggles can fhake off. With *more deliberation*, the *Dutch* erected a ftadholderfhip, that hath been of fignal fervice to their ftate.

THAT excellent hiftorian and ftatefman *Tacitus*, whofe political reflexions are fo juftly and univerfally admired, makes an obfervation in his third annal, that feems to confirm thefe remarks. Having mentioned a worthy man of great abilities, whofe ambitious ardour hurried him into ruin, he ufes thefe words, " *quod multos etiam bonos peffum dedit, qui, fpretis quæ tarda cum fecuritate, præmatura vel cum exitio pro- ; rat.*" " Which misfortune hath happened to many good men, who defpifing thofe things which
they

they might *flowly* and *fafely* attain, fire them too haftily, and with fatal fpeed rufh upon their own deftruction."

If then, Sir, the beft intentions may be difappointed by too rapid a profecution of them, many reafons induce me to think, that this is not the *proper time* to attempt the change of our government.

It is too notorious and too melancholy a truth, that we now labour under the difadvantage of royal and minifterial difpleafure. The conduct of this province, during the late war, hath been almoft continually condemned at home. We have been covered with the reproaches of men, whofe ftations give us juft caufe to regard their reproaches. The laft letters from his majefty's fecretary of ftate prove, that the reputation of the province has not yet revived. We are therein exprefsly charged with double dealing, difrefpect for his Majefty's orders, and, in fhort, accufations, that fhew us to be in the utmoft difcredit. Have we the leaft reafon to believe, when the tranfactions of this year, and the caufe of our application for a change, are made known to the king and his minifters, that their refentment will be waved ? Let us not flatter ourfelves. Will they not be more incenfed, when they find the public fervice impeded, and his majefty's dominions fo long expofed to the ravages of mercilefs enemies, by our inactivity and obftinacy, as it will be faid ? For this, I think, hath been the conftant language of the miniftry on the like occafions. Will not their indignation rife beyond all bounds, when they underftand that our hitherto denying to grant fupplies, and our application for a change, proceed from the governor's ftrict adherence to the terms of the ftipulations, fo folemnly made, and fo repeatedly approved, by the late and prefent King ?

But

BUT I may perhaps be anfwered, " that we have agreed to the terms of the ftipulations, according to their true meaning, which the Governor refufes to do." Surely, Sir, it will require no flight fagacity in diftinguifhing, no common force of argument, to perfuade his Majefty and his Council, that the refufal to comply with the true meaning of the ftipulations proceeds from the Governor, when he infifts on inferting in our bill the very words and letters of thofe ftipulations.

" BUT thefe ftipulations were never intended to be inferted *verbatim* in our bills, and our conftruction is the moft juft." I grant it appears fo to *us*, but much I doubt, whether his Majefty's Council will be of the fame opinion. That Board and this Houfe have often differed as widely in their fentiments. *Our* judgment is founded on the knowledge we have of facts, and of the purity of our intentions. The judgment of *others*, is founded on the reprefentations made to them, of thofe facts and intentions. Thefe reprefentations may be unjuft ; and therefore the decifions that are formed upon them, may be erroneous. If we are rightly informed, we are reprefented as the mortal enemies of the proprietors, who would tear their eftates to pieces, unlefs fome limit was fixed to our fury. For *this purpofe* the fecond and third articles of the ftipulations were formed. The inequality of the mode was explained and enlarged upon by the provincial council ; but in vain. I think, I have heard a worthy member, who lately returned from *England*, mention thefe circumftances.

IF this be the cafe, what reafonable hope can we entertain, of a more favourable determination *now ?* The Proprietors are ftill living. Is it not highly probable that they have intereft enough, either to prevent the change, or to make it on fuch terms, as will fix
upon

upon us *for ever*, thofe demands that appear fo extremely juft to the *prefent Minifters?* One of the Proprietors appears to have great intimacy and influence, with fome very confiderable members of his Majefty's Council. Many men of the higheft character, if public reports fpeak truth, are now endeavring to eftablifh proprietary governments, and therefore probably may be more readily inclined to favour proprietary meafures. The very gentlemen who *formed* the articles of the ftipulations, *are now in power*, and no doubt will inforce their *own Acts* in the ftricteft manner. On the other hand, every circumftance that now operates againft us, may in time turn in our favour. We may perhaps be fortunate enough to fee the prefent prejudices againft us, worn off: to recommend ourfelves to our Sovereign: and to procure the efteem of fome of his minifters. I think I may venture to affert, that fuch a period will be infinitely more proper than the prefent, for attempting a change of government.

WITH the permiffion of the Houfe, I will now confider the *manner* in which this attempt is carried on; and I muft acknowledge, that I do not in the leaft degree approve of it.

THE time may come, when the weight of this government may grow too heavy for the fhoulder of a fubject; at leaft, too heavy for thofe of a woman, or an infant. The proprietary family may be fo circumftanced, as to be willing to accept of fuch an equivalent for the government from the crown, as the crown may be willing to give. Whenever this point is agitated, either on a propofal from the crown or proprietors, this province may plead the caufe of her privileges with greater freedom, and with greater probability of fuccefs, than at prefent The royal grant; the charter founded upon it; the public faith pledged

to

to the adventurers, for the fecurity of thofe rights to
them and their pofterity, whereby they were encouraged to combat the dangers, I had almoft faid, of
another world, to eftablifh the Britifh power in re-
moteft regions, and add ineftimable dominions with
the moft extenfive commerce to their native country;
the high value and veneration we have for thefe privileges; the afflicting lofs and misfortune we fhould
efteem it, to be deprived of them, and the unhap-
pinefs in which his majefty's faithful fubjects in this
province would thereby be involved; our inviolable
loyalty and attachment to his Majefty's perfon and
illuftrious family, whofe fovereignty hath been fo
fingularly diftinguifhed by its favourable influence on
the liberties of mankind.——ALL thefe things may
then be properly infifted on. If urged with that
modeft heart-felt energy, with which good men fhould
always vindicate the interefts of their country before
the beft of fovereigns, I fhould not defpair of a gracious attention, to our humble requefts. Our petition
in fuch a cafe, would be fimple, refpectful, and perhaps affecting.

But in the prefent mode of proceeding, it feems
to me, that we preclude ourfelves from every office
of decent duty to the moft excellent of Kings; and
from that right of earneftly defending our privileges,
which we fhould otherwife have. The foundation
of this attempt, I am apprehenfive, will appear to
others, *peculiarly unfortunate.* In a fudden paffion, it
will be faid, againft the proprietors, we call out for a
change of government. Not from reverence for his
Majefty; not from a fenfe of his paternal goodnefs
to his people; but becaufe we are angry with the
Proprietors; and tired of a difpute founded on an
order approved by his Majefty, and his royal grand-
father.

Our

Our powerful friends on the other fide of the *Atlantic*, who are fo apt to put the kindeft conftructions on our actions, will no doubt obferve, " that the conduct of the people of *Pennfylvania* muft be influenced by very extraordinary councils, fince they defire to come *more immediately* under the King's command, because they will *not obey* thofe royal commands, which have been already fignified to them."

But here it will be faid ; nay it has been faid ; and the petition before the Houfe is drawn accordingly ; " we will not alledge this difpute with the Governor on the ftipulations, but the general inconveniences of a proprietary government, as the caufe of our defiring a change." 'Tis true we may act in this artful manner ; but what advantages fhall we gain by it ? Though *we* fhould keep the fecret, can we feal up the lips of the Proprietors ? Can we recal our meffages to the Governor ? Can we annihilate our own refolves ? Will not all——will not any of thefe difcover the *true caufe* of the prefent attempt ?

Why then, fhould we unneceffarily invite frefh invectives in the very beginning of a moft important bufinefs, that to be happily concluded, requires all the favour we can procure, and all the dexterity we can practice ?

We intend to furround the throne, with petitions that our government may be changed from proprietary to royal. At the fame time we mean to preferve our privileges : But how are thefe two points to be reconciled ?

If we exprefs our defire for the prefervation of our privileges, in fo general or faint a manner as may induce the King to think they are of no great confe-

quence

quence to us, it will be nothing lefs than to betray our country.

If, on the other hand, we inform his Majefty, " that though we *requeft* him to change the government, yet we *infift* on the prefervation of our privileges," certainly it will be thought an unprecedented Stile of petitioning the crown, that humbly afks a favour, and boldly prefcribes the terms, on which it muft be granted.

How then fhall we act ? Shall we fpeak, or fhall we fupprefs our fentiments ? The firft method will render our requeft incoherent : the fecond will render it dangerous.   Some gentlemen are of opinion, that thefe difficulties may be folved, by intrufting the management of this affair to an Agent : but I fee no reafon to expect fuch an effect. I would firft obferve that this matter is of too prodigious confequence to be trufted to the difcretion of an Agent. ——But if it fhall be committed by this Houfe, *the proper guardian of the public liberties*, to *other* hands, this truth muft at fome time or other be difclofed, " that we will never confent to a change, unlefs our privileges are preferved." I fhould be glad to know, with what fineffe this matter is to be conducted. Is the agent to keep our petition to the crown in his pocket, till he has whifpered to the miniftry ? Will this be juftifiable ? Will it be decent ? Whenever he applies to *them*, I prefume, they will defire to know his authority for making fuch an application. Then our petition muft appear ; and whenever it does appear, either at firft or laft, *that*, and the others tranfmitted with it, I apprehend, will be the foundation of any refolutions taken in the King's Council.

Thus, in whatever view this tranfaction is confidered, fhall we not ftill be involved in the dilemma already

ready mentioned, " of begging a favour from his Majefty's goodnefs, and yet fhewing a diftruft that the
royal hand, ftretched out at our own requeft for our
relief, may do us an injury ?"

LET me fuppofe, and none can offer the leaft proof
of this fuppofition being unreafonable, that his Majefty will not accept of the government, clog'd, as it
will be faid, with privileges inconfiftent with the royal
rights : how fhall we act then ? We fhall have our
choice of two things ; one of them deftructive : the
other difhonourable. We may either renounce the
laws and liberties framed and delivered down to us
by our careful anceftors : or we may tell his Majefty,
with a furly difcontent, " that we will not fubmit to
his *implored protection*, but on fuch conditions, as we
pleafe to impofe on him." Is not this the inevitable
and dreadful alternative, to which we fhall reduce ourfelves ?

IN fhort, Sir, I think the farther we advance in
the path we are now in, the greater will be the confufion and danger in which we fhall engage ourfelves.
Any body of men acting under a charter muft furely
tread on flippery ground, when they take a ftep that
may be deemed a furrender of that charter. For my
part, I think the petitions that have been carried
about the city and country to be figned, and are now
lying on the table, can be regarded in no other light,
than as a furrender of the charter, with a fhort in-
different hint annexed of a defire, that our privileges
may be fpared, if it fhall be thought proper. Many
ftriking arguments may in my opinion be urged, to
prove that any requeft made by this Houfe for a
change, may with ftill greater propriety be called a
furrender. The common obfervation " that many of
our privileges do not depend on our charter only, but
are confirmed by laws approved by the Crown," I

doubt

doubt will have but little weight with thofe, who will determine this matter.

I⟶ will readily be replied, " that thefe laws were founded' on the charter ; that they were calculated for a proprietary government, and for no other; and approved by the Crown in that view alone : that the proprietary government is now acknowledged by the people living under it to be a bad government ; and the Crown is intreated to accept a furrender of it : that therefore, by abolifhing the proprietary government, every thing founded upon it muft of confequence be alfo abolifhed."

However, if there fhould be any doubts in the law on thefe points, there is an eafy way to folve them.

These reflexions, Sir, naturally lead me to confider the *confequences* that may attend a change of government ; which is the laft point, I fhall trouble the Houfe upon at this time.

It is not to be queftioned, but that the Miniftry are defirous of vefting the immediate government of this Province, advantageoufly in the Crown. 'Tis true, they don't chufe to act arbitrarily, and tear away the prefent government from us, without our confent. This is not the age for fuch things. But let *us* only furnifh them with a pretext, by prefling petitions for a change ; let 'us only relinquifh the hold we now have, and in an inftant we are precipitated from that envied height where we now ftand. The affair is laid before the Parliament, the defires of the Miniftry are infinuated, the rights of the Crown are vindicated, and an act pafles to deliver us at once from the government of Proprietors, and the privileges we claim under them.

THEN

THEN, Sir, we who *in particular* have prefented to the authors of the fatal change, this *long-wifh'd* for opportunity of effecting it, fhall for *our affiftance* be entitled to their thanks —— *Thanks !* which, I am perfuaded, every worthy member of this Houfe would *abhor* to deferve, and would *fcorn* to receive.

IT feems to be taken for granted, that, by a change of government, we fhall obtain a change of thofe meafures which are fo difpleafing to the people of this Province —— that juftice will be maintained by an equal taxation of the proprietary eftates —— and that our frequent diffenfions will be turned into peace and happinefs.

THESE are effects indeed fincerely to be wifhed for by every fenfible, by every honeft man : but reafon does not always teach us to expect the warm wifhes of the heart. Could our gracious Sovereign take into confideration, the ftate of every part of his extended dominions, we *might* expect redrefs of every grievance: for with the moft implicit conviction I believe, he is as juft, benevolent, and amiable a Prince, as Heaven ever granted in its mercy to blefs a people. I venerate his virtues beyond all expreffion. But *his* atttention to our particular circumftances being impoffible, we muft receive our fate from minifters ; and from *them*, I do not like to receive it.

WE are not the fubjects of minifters ; and therefore it is not to be wondered at, if they do not feel that tendernefs for us, that a good prince will always feel for his people. Men are not born minifters. Their ambition raifes them to authority ; and when poffeffed of it, one eftablifhed principle with them feems to be, " never to deviate from a precedent of power."

DID

Did we not find in the late war, though we exerted
ourselves in the moſt active manner in the defence of
his Majeſty's dominions, and in promoting the ſervice
of the Crown, every point, in which the Proprietors
thought fit to make any oppoſition, decided againſt
us ? Have we not alſo found, ſince the laſt diſturbance
of the public peace by our ſavage enemies, the conduct of the late Governor highly applauded by the
miniſtry, for his adherence to thoſe very ſtipulations
now inſiſted on; and ourſelves ſubjected to the *bittereſt
reproaches*, only for attempting to avoid burthens,
that were thought extremely grievous. Other inſtances
of the like kind I paſs over, to avoid a tedious reca-
pitulation.

Since then, the gale of miniſterial favour has in *all
ſeaſons* blown propitious to proprietary intereſt, why
do we now fondly flatter ourſelves, that it will *ſuddenly*
ſhift its quarter ? Why ſhould we, with an *amazing
credulity*, now fly for *protection* to *thoſe* men, truſt *every
thing* to *their* mercy, and aſk the moſt diſtinguiſhing
favours from *their* kindneſs, from whom we com-
plained, a few months ago, that we could not obtain
the moſt reaſonable requeſts ? Surely, Sir, we muſt
acknowledge one of theſe two things : either, that
our *complaint* was then *unjuſt* ; or, that our *confidence*
is now *unwarranted*. For my part, I look for a rigid
perſeverance in former meaſures. With a new government, I expect new diſputes. The experience of
the royal colonies convinces me, that the immediate
government of the Crown, is not a ſecurity for that
tranquillity and happineſs we promiſe ourſelves from a
change. It is needleſs for me to remind the Houſe,
of all the frequent and violent controverſies that have
happened between the King's Governors in ſeveral
provinces, and their Aſſemblies. At this time, if I
am rightly informed, *Virginia* is ſtruggling againſt an
inſtruction relating to their paper currency, that will
be

be attended, as that colony apprehends, with the moſt
deſtructive conſequences, if carried into execution.

INDEED, Sir, it ſeems vain to expect, where the
ſpirit of liberty is maintained among a people, that
public conteſts ſhould not *alſo* be maintained. Thoſe
who *govern*, and thoſe who *are governed*, ſeldom think
they can gain too much on one another. Power is like
the *ocean* ; not eaſily admitting limits to be fixed in it.
It muſt be in motion. Storms indeed are not de-
ſirable : but a long dead calm is not to be looked for ;
perhaps, not to be wiſhed for. Let not *us* then, in
expectation of *ſmooth ſeas*, and an *undiſturbed courſe*, too
raſhly venture our *little veſſel* that hath ſafely ſailed
round *our own well known* ſhores, upon the *midſt* of
the *untry'd deep*, without being firſt fully convinced,
that her *make* is ſtrong enough to bear the *weather* ſhe
may meet with, and that ſhe is well *provided* for ſo
long and ſo dangerous a voyage.

No man, Sir, amongſt us hath denied, or will deny,
that this Province muſt *ſtake*, on the event of the
preſent attempt, liberties that ought to be immortal.
—— *Liberties !* founded on the acknowledged rights
of human nature ; and reſtrained in our mother-
country, only by an unavoidable neceſſity of adhering,
in ſome meaſure, to long eſtabliſhed cuſtoms. Thus
hath been formed between old errors and haſty inno-
vations, an entangled chain, that our anceſtors either
had not moderation or leiſure enough to untwiſt.

I WILL now briefly enumerate, as well as I can recollect, the particular privileges of *Pennſylvania*.

IN the firſt place, we here enjoy that beſt and
greateſt of all rights, *a perfect religious freedom*.

POSTS

Posts of honour and profit are unfettered with *oaths* or *tests*; and therefore are open to men, whofe abilities, ftrict regard to their confcientious perfuafion, and unblemifhed characters, qualify them to difcharge their duties with credit to themfelves, and advantage to their country. Thus juftice is done to merit; and the public lofes none of its able fervants.

The fame wifdom of our laws has guarded againft the abfurdity of granting greater credit even to villains, if they will fwear, than to men of virtue, who from religious motives cannot. Therefore thofe who are confcientioufly fcrupulous of taking an oath are admitted as witneffes in criminal cafes. Our legiflation fuffers no checks, from a council inftituted, in fancied imitation of the Houfe of Lords. By the right of fitting on our own adjournments, we are fecure of meeting, when the public good requires it: and of not being difmift, when private paffions demand it. At the fame time, the ftrict difcharge of the truft committed to Us, is inforced by the fhort duration of our power, which muft be renewed by our conftituents every year.

Nor are the people ftript of all authority, in the execution of laws. They enjoy the fatisfaction of having fome fhare, by the appointment of provincial commiffioners, in laying out the money which they raife; and of being in this manner affured, that it is applied to the purpofes, for which it was granted. They alfo elect fheriffs and coroners; officers of fo much confequence, in every determination that affects honour, liberty, life, or property.

Let any impartial perfon reflect, how contradictory fome of thefe privileges are to the moft antient principles of the Englifh conftitution, and how directly oppofite others of them are to the fettled prerogatives
of

of the crown; and then confider, what probability we have of retaining them on a *requefted* * change : that is, of continuing in fact a proprietary government, though we humbly pray the King to change this government. Not unaptly, in my opinion, the connexion between the proprietary family and this Province, may be regarded as a marriage. Our privileges may be called the fruits of that marriage. The domeftic peace of this family, it is true, has not been unvexed with quarrels and complaints : But the pledges of their affection ought always to be efteemed : and whenever the parents on an *imprudent requeft* fhall be *divorced*, much I fear, that their *iffue* will be declared *illegitimate*. ———— *This* I am well perfuaded of, that furprizing muft our behaviour appear to all men, if, in the inftant when we apply to his Majefty for relief from what we think oppreffion, we fhould difcover a refolute difpofition to deprive him of the uncontroverted prerogatives of his royal dignity.

At this period, when the adminiftration is regulating new colonies, and defigning, as we are told, the † *ftricteft reformations* in the old, it is not likely that they will grant an invidious diftinction in our favour. Lefs likely is it, as that diftinction will be liable to fo many, and fuch ftrong *conftitutional* objections ; and when we fhall have the weight both of the clergy and miniftry, and the univerfally-received opinions of the people of our mother country to contend with.

I mean not, Sir, the leaft reflexion on the church of *England*. I reverence and admire the purity of its doctrine, and the moderation of its temper. I am

---

* *Imperium facile iis artibus retinetur, quibus initio partum eft.*
                                        Sall. Bell. Catalin.
† Some late Acts of Parliament fhew what ftrict reformations are to be made in the Colonies.

convinced

convinced, that it is filled with learned and with excellent men : but all zealous perfons think their own religious tenets the beft, and would willingly fee them embraced by others. I therefore apprehend, that the dignified and reverend gentlemen of the church of *England*, will be extremely defirous to have *that* church as well fecured, and as much diftinguifh-.ed as poffible, in the *American* colonies : efpecially in thofe colonies, where it is overborne, as it were, by diffenters. There never can be a more critical opportunity for this purpofe than the prefent. The caufe of the church will befides be connected with that of the crown, to which its principles are thought to be more favourable, than thofe of the other profeffions.

We have received certain information, that the conduct of this Province, which has been fo much cenfured by the miniftry, is attributed to the influence of a fociety, that holds warlike meafures at all times to be unlawful. ——— We alfo know, that the late tumultuous and riotous proceedings, which are reprefented in fo ftrong a light by the petition now before the Houfe, have been publicly afcribed to the influence of another fociety. Thus the blame of every thing difreputable to this province is caft on one or the other of thefe diffenting fects. Circumftances ! that I imagine, will neither be forgot, nor neglected.

We have feen the event of our difputes concerning the *Proprietary* interefts ; and it is not to be expected, that our fuccefs will be greater when our opponents become more numerous ; and will have more dignity, more power, and, as they will think, more law on their fide.

THESE

.These are the dangers, Sir, to which we are now about to expofe thofe privileges, in which we have hitherto fo much gloried. *Wherefore?* To procure two or three, perhaps four or five hundred pounds a year (for no calculation has carried the fum higher) from the Proprietors, for two or three or four or five years; for fo long, and fomething longer perhaps, the taxes may continue.

But are we fure of gaining this point? *We are not* Are we fure of gaining any other advantage? *We are not.* Are we fure of preferving our privileges? *We are not.* Are we under a neceffity of purfuing the meafure propofed at this time? *We are not.*

Here, Sir, permit me to make a fhort Paufe. — Permit me to appeal to the heart of every member in this Houfe, and to entreat him to reflect, how far he can be juftifiable in giving his voice, thus to hazard the liberties fecured to us by the wife founders of this Province; peaceably and fully enjoyed by the prefent age, and to which pofterity is fo juftly entitled.

But, Sir, we are told there is no danger of lofing our privileges, if our government fhould be changed; and two arguments are ufed in fupport of this opinion. —— The firft is, " That the government of the Crown is exercifed with fo much lenity in *Carolina* and the *Jerfeys.*"——I cannot perceive the leaft degree of force in this argument. As to *Carolina*, I am not a little furprized, that it fhould be mentioned on this occafion, fince I never heard of one privilege that colony enjoys, more than all the other royal governments in *America.* The privileges of the *Jerfeys* are of a different nature from many of which we are poffeft; and are more confiftent with the royal prerogative.

Indeed

INDEED I know of none they have, except that *Quakers* may be witnesses in criminal cases, and may bear offices. Can this indulgence, shewn to them for a particular reason, and not contradictory to the rights of the crown, give us any just cause to expect the confirmation of privileges directly opposite to those rights ; and for confirming which, no such reason exists. But perhaps the gentlemen, who advance this argument, mean, that *we* shall purchase a change at a cheap price, if we are only reduced to the same state with the *Jerseys*——Surely, Sir, if this be their meaning, they entirely forget those extraordinary privileges, which some time ago were mentioned.

How many must we in such a case renounce! I apprehend, it would prove an argument of little consolation to these gentlemen, if they should lose three-fourths of their estates, to be told, that they still remain as rich as their neighbours, and have enough to procure all the necessaries of life.

IT is somewhat remarkable, that this single instance of favour in permitting an affirmation instead of an oath, in a single province, should be urged as so great an encouragement to us, while there are so many examples of another kind to deterr us. In what *royal government* besides the *Jerseys*, can a *Quaker* be a witness in criminal cases, and bear offices *(a)* ? *In no other.* What can be the reason of this distinction in the *Jerseys?* Because in the infancy of that colony, when it came under the government of the crown, there was, as appears from authentic vouchers, an ABSOLUTE NECESSITY, from the scarcity of other proper persons, to make use of the people called

(a) It is said, that a Quaker was lately committed to goal in *New-York*, because he would not swear in a criminal case.

Quakers

Quakers in public employments. Is there such a necessity in this Province ? Or can the miniftry be *perfuaded*, that there is fuch a neceffity ? No, Sir, thofe from whom they will receive their information, will grant no fuch thing ; and therefore I think there is the *moft imminent danger*, in cafe of a change, that the people of *this fociety* will lofe the exercife of thofe rights, which though they are intitled to as men, yet fuch is the fituation of human affairs, they with difficulty can find a fpot on the whole globe where they are allowed to enjoy them. It will be an argument of fome force, I am afraid, that the church of *England* can never expect to raife its head among us, while we are encouraged, as it will be faid, in diffention : but if an *oath* be made neceffary for obtaining offices of honour and profit ; it will then be expected that any Quakers, who are tempted to renounce their principles, will undoubtedly make an addition to the eftablifhed church.

IF any other confideration than that which has been mentioned was regarded in granting that indulgence in the *Jerfeys*, though no other is expreft, it feems not improbable, that the nearnefs of this Province might have had fome weight, as from its fituation it afforded fuch ftrong temptations to the inhabitants of the *Jerfeys* to remove hither, had they been treated with any feverity.

THEIR government in fome meafure was formed in imitation of our government ; but when this is altered, the *Englifh* conftitution muft be the model, by which it will be formed.

HERE it will be faid, " this cannot be done but by the Parliament ; and will a Britifh Parliament do fuch an act of injuftice, as to deprive us of our rights ?"

This

This is the fecond argument, ufed to prove the fafety of the meafures now propofed.

CERTAINLY the *Britifh* Parliament will not do, what they think, an unjuft act : but I cannot perfuade my-felf, that *they* will think it unjuft, to place us on the fame footing with themfelves. It will not be an eafy tafk to convince them, that the people of *Pennfylvania* ought to be diftinguifhed from all other fubjects, under his Majefty's *immediate* government ; or that fuch a diftinction can anfwer any good purpofe. May it not be expected, that they will fay, " No people " can be freer than ourfelves ; every thing more than " we enjoy, is licentioufnefs, not liberty : any in- " dulgencies fhewn to the colonies heretofore, were " like the indulgencies of parents to their infants ; " they ought to ceafe with that tender age ; and, as " the colonies grow up to a more vigorous ftate, " they ought to be carefully difciplined, and all their " actions regulated by ftrict laws. Above all things " it is neceffary, that the prerogative fhould be exer- " cifed with its full force in our American provinces, " to reftrain them within due bounds, and fecure " their dependance on this kingdom."

I AM afraid, that this will be the opinion of the Parliament, as it has been, in every inftance, the unde-viating practice of the Miniftry.

BUT, Sir, it may be faid, " thefe reafons are not " conclufive, they do not demonftratively prove, that " our privileges *will be* endangered by a change." I grant the objection : but what ftronger reafons, what clearer proofs are there, that they *will not be* endanger-ed by a change.

THEY are fafe now ; and *why* fhould we engage in an enterprize that will render them *uncertain?* if nothing

thing will content us but a revolution brought about by ourfelves, furely we ought to have made the ftrict-eft enquiries what terms we may expect; and to have obtained from the miniftry fome kind of fecurity for the performance of thofe terms.

THESE things might have been done. They are not done. If a merchant will venture to travel with great riches into a foreign country, without a proper guide, it certainly will be advifeable for him to pro-cure the beft intelligence he can get, of the climate, the roads, the difficulties he will meet with, and the treatment he may receive.

I PRAY the Houfe to confider, if we have the flight-eft fecurity that can be mentioned, except opinion (if that is any) either for the prefervation of our prefent privileges, or gaining a fingle advantage from a change. Have we any writing? have we a verbal promife from any Minifter of the Crown? We have not. I cannot therefore conceal my aftonifhment, that gentlemen fhould require a lefs fecurity for the invaluable rights of *Pennfylvania*, than they would demand for a debt of five pounds. Why fhould we prefs forward with this unexampled hurry, when no benefit can be derived from it? Why fhould we have any averfion to deliberation and delay, when no injury can attend them?

It is fcarcely poffible, in the prefent cafe, that we can fpend too much time, in forming refolutions, the confequences of which are to be *perpetual*. If it is true, as fome averr, that we can *now* obtain an advan-tageous change of government, I fuppofe it will be alfo true next week, next month, and next year: but if *they* are miftaken, it will be early enough, whenever it happens, to be difappointed, and to repent. I am not willing to run rifques in a matter of fuch pro-

4   digious

digious importance, on the credit of *any man's opinion*, when by a fmall delay, that can do no harm, the fteps we are to take may become more fafe. *Gideon*, though he had converfed with an " angel of the lord," would not attempt to relieve his countrymen, then forely oppreft by the *Midianites*, leaft he fhould involve them in greater miferies, until he was convinced by two miracles that he fhould be fuccefsful. I do not fay, we ought to wait for *miracles*; but I think we ought to wait for fomething, which will be next kin to a miracle; I mean, fome *fign* of a *favourable dif-pofition* in the *miniftry* toward us. I fhould like to fee an *olive leaf* at leaft brought to us, before we quit the *ark*.

Permit me, Sir, to make one propofal to the Houfe. We may apply to the Crown now, as freely as if we were under its immediate government. Let us defire his Majefty's judgment on the point, that has ocafioned this unhappy difference between the two branches of the legiflature. This may be done with-out any * violence, without any hazard to our con-ftitution. We fay, the juftice of our demands is clear as light : every heart muft feel the equity of them.

If the decifion be in our favour, we gain a confi-derable victory ; the grand obftruction of the public fervice is removed ; and we fhall have more leifure to carry our intentions coolly into execution. If the de-cifion be againft us, I believe the moft zealous amongft us will grant it would be madnefs to expect fuccefs in any other conteft. This will be a fingle point, and cannot meet with fuch difficulties, as the procuring a total alteration of the government. There-fore, by feparating it from other matters, we fhall

---

* Nihil vi, nihil feceffione opus eft.   Sall. Bell. Jugurth.

foon obtain a determination, and know *what chance we* have of fucceeding in things of greater value. Let us try our fortune. Let us take a caft or two of the dice for fmaller matters, before we dip deeply. Few gamefters are of fo fanguine a temper, as to ftake their *whole wealth* on *one* defperate throw at firft. If we *are* to *play* with the *public happinefs*, let us act at leaft with *as much* deliberation, as if we were *betting* out of our private purfes.

PERHAPS a little delay may afford us the pleafure of finding our conftituents more unanimous in their opinions on this interefting occafion : and I fhould chufe to fee a vaft majority of them join with a calm refolution in the meafure, before I fhould think myfelf juftifiable in voting for it, even if I approved of it.

THE prefent queftion is utterly foreign from the purpofes, for which we were fent into this place. There was not the leaft probability at the time we were elected, that this matter could come under our confideration. We are not debating how much money we fhall raife : what laws we fhall pafs for the regulation of property ; nor on any thing of the fame kind that arifes in the ufual parliamentary courfe of bufinefs. We are now to determine, WHETHER A STEP SHALL BE TAKEN, THAT MAY PRODUCE AN ENTIRE CHANGE OF OUR CONSTITUTION.

IN forming this determination, one ftriking reflexion fhould be preferved in our minds ; I mean, " that we are the fervants of the people of *Pennfilvania*," —— of *that people*, who have been induced, by the excellence of the prefent conftitution, to fettle themfelves under its Protection.

THE

THE inhabitants of remote countries, impelled by that love of liberty which All-wife Providence has planted in the human heart, deferting their native foils, committed themfelves with their helplefs families to the mercy of winds and waves, and braved all the terrors of an unknown wildernefs, in hopes of enjoying in thefe woods the exercife of thofe invaluable rights, which fome unhappy circumftance had denied to mankind in every other part of the earth.

THUS, Sir, the people of *Pennfylvania* may be faid to have *purchafed* an inheritance in its conftitution, at a prodigious price ; and I cannot believe, unlefs the ftrongeft evidence be offered, that they are now willing to part with that, which has coft them fo much toil and expence.

THEY have not hitherto been difappointed in their wifhes. They have obtained the bleffings they fought for.

WE have received thefe feats by the free choice of this people, under this conftitution ; and to preferve it in its utmoft purity and vigour, has always been deemed by me, a principal part of the truft committed to my care and fidelity. The meafure now propofed has a direct tendency to endanger this conftitution : and therefore, in my opinion, we have *no right* to engage in it, without the *almoft univerfal confent of the people*, expreft in the plaineft manner.

I THINK, I fhould improperly employ the attention of this Houfe, if I fhould take up much time in proving, that the deputies of a people have not a right, by any law divine or human, to change the government under which their authority was delegated to them, without fuch a confent as has been mentioned.——The pofition is fo confonant to natural juftice and common fenfe, that I believe it

3   uever

never has been been ſeriouſly controverted. All the learned authors that I recollect to have mentioned this matter, ſpeak of it as an indiſputable maxim.

It may be (b) ſaid, perhaps, in anſwer to this objection, " that it is not intended to change the government, but the governor." This, I apprehend, is a diſtinction only in words. The government is certainly to be changed from proprietary to royal ; and *whatever may be intended*, the queſtion is, whether ſuch a change will not expoſe our preſent privileges to danger.

It may alſo be ſaid, " that the petitions lying on the table, are a proof of the people's conſent." Can petitions ſo induſtriouſly carried about, and, after all the pains taken, ſigned only by about thirty-five hundred perſons, be looked on as the *plaineſt expreſſions of the almoſt univerſal conſent* of the many thouſands that fill this Province ? No one can believe it.

It cannot be denied, Sir, that much the greateſt part of the inhabitants of this Province, and among them men of large fortunes, good ſenſe, and fair characters, who value very highly the intereſt they have in the preſent conſtitution, have not ſigned theſe petitions ; and, as there is reaſon to apprehend, are extremely averſe to a change at this time. Will they not complain of ſuch a change ? And if it is not attended with all the advantages they now enjoy, will they not have reaſon to complain ? It is not improbable, that this meaſure may lay the foundation of more bitter, and more laſting diſſentions among us, than any we have yet experienced.

Before I cloſe this catalogue of unhappy conſequences, that I expect will follow our requeſt of a

(b) This was frequently ſaid in the Houſe.

D 2   change,

change, I beg leave to take notice of the *terms* of the petition, that is now under· the confideration of the Houfe. ·

THEY equally excite in my breaft —— furprize, and grief, and terror. This poor province is already finking under the weight of the difcredit, and reproaches, that by *fome fatality*, for feveral years paft, have attended our public meafures; and we not only feize this unfortunate feafon to engage her in new difficulties, but prepare to pour on her devoted head, a load that muft effectually crufh her. —— We inform the King, by this petition, that *Pennfylvania* is become a fcene of confufion and anarchy: that armed mobs are marching from one place to another: that fuch a fpirit of violence and riot prevails, as expofes his Majefty's good fubjects to conftant alarms and danger: and that this tumultuous difpofition is fo general, that it cannot be controuled by any powers of the prefent government; and that we have not any hopes of returning to a ftate of peace and fafety, but by being taken under his Majefty's immediate protection.

I CANNOT think this a proper reprefentation of the prefent ftate of this Province. Near four months are elapfed, fince the laft riot: and I do not perceive the leaft probability of our being troubled with any more. The rioters were not only fuccefsfully oppofed, and prevented from executing their purpofe; but we have reafon to believe, that they were convinced of their error, and have renounced all thoughts of fuch wild attempts for the future. To whofe threat is the fword now held? What life will be faved by this application? Imaginary danger! Vain remedy! Have we not *fufficiently felt* the effects of royal refentment? Is not the authority of the Crown *fully enough exerted* over us, does it become *us* to paint, in the ftrongeft colours, the folly or the crimes of our *countrymen?*

To

To require unneceffary protection, againft men who intend us no injury, in fuch *loofe* and *general* expreffions, *as may produce even the eftablifhment of an armed force among us ?*

WITH unremitting vigilance, with undaunted vir-tue, fhould a free people *watch* againft the encroach-ments of power, and *remove* every pretext for its ex-tenfion,

W E are a dependant colony; and we need not doubt, that means will be ufed to fecure that de-pendance. But that we ourfelves fhould furnifh a reafon for fettling a *military eftablifhment* upon us, muft exceed the moft extravagant wifhes of thofe, who would be moft pleafed with fuch a meafure.

W E may introduce the innovation, but we fhall not be able to ftop its progrefs. The precedent will be pernicious. If a fpecious pretence is afforded for maintaining a fmall body of troops among us now, equally fpecious pretences will never be wanting here-after, for adding to their numbers, The burthen that will be impofed on us for their fupport, is the moft trifling part of the evil. The poifon will foon reach our vitals. Whatever ftruggles we may make to expell it,

Hæret lateri lethalis arundo ——

THE dart with which we are ftruck, will ftill re-main fixed——too firmly fixed, for our feeble hands to draw it out. Our fruitlefs efforts will but irritate the wound; and at length we muft tamely fubmit to —— I quit a fubject too painful to be dwelt upon.

THESE

THESE, Sir, are my sentiments on the petition that has occasioned this debate. I think this neither the *proper season*, nor the *proper method*, for obtaining a change of our government. It is *uncertain*; whether the measures proposed will place us in a better situation, than we are now in, with regard to the point lately controverted : with respect to other particulars, it may place us in a worse. We shall run the *risque* of *suffering* great *losses*. We have *no certainty* of *gaining* any thing. In seeking a *precarious, hasty, violent* remedy for the present *partial* disorder, we are *sure* of exposing the *whole body* to danger. I cannot perceive the necessity of aplying such a remedy. If I did, I would with the greatest pleasure pass over to the opinion of some gentlemen who differ from me, whose integrity and abilities I so much esteem, that, whatever reasons at any time influence me to agree with them, I always receive a satisfaction from being on their side. If I have erred now, I shall comfort myself with reflecting, that it is an *innocent error*. Should the measures pursued in consequence of this debate be opposite to my opinion ; and should they procure a change of government with all the benefits we desire; I shall not envy the praise of others, who, by their *fortunate* courage and skill, have conducted us unhurt, through the midst of such threatening dangers, to the wished-for port. I shall chearfully submit to the censure of having been *too apprehensive* of injuring the people of this Province. If any severer sentence shall be passed upon me by the worthy, I shall be sorry for it : but this truth I am convinced of ; that it will be much easier for me to bear the unmerited reflexions of *mistaken zeal*, than the just reproaches of a *guilty mind*. To have concealed my real sentiments, or to have counterfeited such as I do not entertain, in a deliberation of *so much consequence* as the present, would have been the *basest hypocrisy*. It may perhaps be thought that this however would have been the most

politic

politic part for me to have acted. It might have been so. But if *policy* requires, that our words or actions should *belye* our hearts, I thank God that I *detest* and *despise* all its *arts*, and all its *advantages*. A good man *ought* to serve his country, even though she *resents* his services. The great reward of honest actions, is not the fame or profit that follows them, but the *consciousness* that attends them. To discharge, on this important occasion, the *inviolable duty* I owe the public, by obeying the *unbiassed dictates* of my *reason* and *conscience*, hath been my sole view; and my only wish now is, that the resolutions of this House, whatever they are, may promote the happiness of *Pennsilvania*.

F I N I S.